WHAT'S IN *Your* BOX?

CHANEL BLACKMORE

Scripture quotations taken from the Holy Bible:
New International Version and Amplified Bible.

Printed in the United States of America

ISBN-13: 978-1721942589

ISBN-10: 1721942580

One of the things that's important in life is that you have a man and woman of God that oversee your spiritual growth. I want to thank God for Pastor and Sister Sharp because they are worthy of all of the praise and honor as their position affords them. I'm also grateful that God let me be a part of this family. For this reading, we'll be looking at John 12:1, and we'll start from there.

Chanel Blackmore

Table of Contents

Foreword

By Coach Dawniel Winningham

What's in your Box?

It took me 40 years to figure out what was in my box. I used to feel bad about it taking so long until I reflected on the Israelites who took 40 years or better to realize their destiny, or others who had to spend an inordinate amount of time to find out what was in their box. The Bible is a great teacher. I don't feel so bad now. Because at least I found it.

So if you are HERE right now, don't worry about how long it took you to get here; instead focus on the fact that you made it. And you made it because God loves you. You are not here by accident.

The first time that I heard Chanel discuss "What's in your box?", I was blown away by how on point she was in showing us JUST how much the Bible prepares us to handle what is in our box.

Each one of your trials and tribulations were not designed to hurt you, but to make you stronger. As you listen and read as Chanel helps you open your box, don't be surprised that you have access to MORE resources than you think you have. You have MORE knowledge than you think you do.

You is KIND, you is STRONG and YOU is Important.

Don't forget that.

It has been a TREAT watching Chanel open her box, and I watch in delight as she helps others. That is why the fellowship of women is so important.

Because what's in MY Box is so heavily dependent upon what's in yours.

Will you open it?

Dawniel Winningham

Master Life and Business Coach
Former Fortune 10 Vice President
Box Opened 7/11/2011

Introduction

What's in your box? Everyone has a box, correct? We'll see what's in yours, and we'll start from John 12:1-8 (New International Version):

> ¹Six days before the Passover, Jesus came to Bethany, where Lazarus lived, whom Jesus had raised from the dead. ²Here a dinner was given in Jesus' honor. Martha served, while Lazarus was among those reclining at the table with him. ³Then Mary took about a pint of pure nard, an expensive perfume; she poured it on Jesus' feet and wiped his feet with her hair. And the house was filled with the fragrance of the perfume.
>
> ⁴But one of his disciples, Judas Iscariot, who was later to betray him, objected, ⁵"Why wasn't this perfume sold and the money given to the poor? It was worth a year's wages." ⁶He did not say this because he cared about the poor but because he was a thief; as keeper of the money bag, he used to help himself to what was put into it.

[7]"Leave her alone," Jesus replied. "It was intended that she should save this perfume for the day of my burial. [8]You will always have the poor among you, but you will not always have me."

What's in your box? In this passage, we find that Jesus is on his way to Bethany to have dinner at Lazarus his house. The scripture says that this is the same Lazarus whom he called from the tomb.

Lazarus, who was Mary and Martha's brother, these where Jesus friends; he loved them and they loved him. During dinner, Mary comes in with a jar or a box of expensive perfume and she anoints Jesus' feet. Let's take a closer look at this; I know a lot of us have heard this scripture before in Sunday school, but I want you to bear with me because I want to look at some things that we might've missed in Sunday school.

Chapter One

The Characteristics of Mary

First, I want to look at Mary. This is the same Mary that opened up her house with Martha to Jesus and his disciples many times. Mary was always the one sitting at Jesus' feet. We Know that Martha served, and was always busy, but Mary sat at the feet of Jesus. She was there when he told about the power of God, and she was there when he talked about the kingdom.

As I stated earlier, Mary was Lazarus's sister and when he got sick, she and Martha sent a message to Jesus. Personally, I like to visualize these things, so I can see Mary listening to Jesus as he talked about the kingdom and the power of God, and I know she witnessed these miracles.

I'd like to think that she sent that message when her brother was sick because she believed Jesus could do what he said he could do. Imagine, she heard him talk about all of these things; she must have known from the hours of listening to Jesus that the power of God and the kingdom was real!

Now that we have a clear picture of who Mary is, let's go back to the scripture of John 12:1-8. It clearly says that Jesus was having dinner at Mary's house after he raised Lazarus from the dead; this happens in the 11th chapter of John, and the Word tells us that this dinner here in Chapter 12 is in honor of Jesus.

And then the scripture says that Mary comes in with a box filled with a rare, expensive perfume. She opens it up and she pours it on Jesus' feet. Once she pours that oil on his feet, she washed them with her hair. I know in another place in the scripture it says with her tears.

I think that's extremely powerful! When I first read that, I couldn't help to think 'that's love'— to get down and pour your oil that you got with hard-earned money, on Jesus' feet. Let's take a closer look at this action.

I know Jesus is God, and I know that He is holy, but his feet were dirty. There's no other way to put it! She didn't care that his feet were dirty. The only thing that she cared about was ministering unto Jesus. No matter what state he was in or his feet, she didn't think about that.

The second thing that comes to mind is that she had little regard for those who are around her or her traditions. Typically, as a Jewish woman, if you let your hair down in a room full of men, you weren't looked upon kindly!

Mary really didn't care at all. Not even from the book of St. John, chapter 10 when she first met Jesus, nor in chapter 11 when she ran out crying because he let her brother die; I'm sure she thought that.

However, she washed his feet with little regard. To be in a room full of men, and be the only woman with your hair down, pouring expensive oil on Jesus' feet and washing them with her hair, it speaks of intimacy. She had to get in close to him. In all honesty, how can one render worship if you're not close to Jesus?

Remember what's in your box!

Mary came boldly to render worship to Jesus. I'll show you something else that I know we didn't see. He allowed her come close. That means that he knew her, that he felt comfortable with her to allow her to come close and render worship unto him. It's intimate.

In order for you to get something from Jesus, you must first know who he is, and who he is to you. In all honesty, Mary DID have a relationship with Jesus; we may only see it in the book of St. John, chapter 11, and a little bit in chapter 10, but they were friends.

The Bible says that he loved them and they loved him. Now that we've got that established, I'd like to ask some questions over the next couple of chapters. You don't have to answer them out loud; just answer them in your head!

~ MOMENT OF REFLECTION ~

How are you like Mary? How will this help you
open your box?

_____

_____

_____

_____

_____

_____

_____

_____

_____

_____

_____

_____

Chapter Two

Who Is Jesus to You?

Let that question sink in, and answer when you can. If you don't know the answer, that's a problem, but that's okay; we'll fix it!

The first thing Jesus should be to you is a friend. Let's look at Proverbs 18:24 (New International Version), it reads:

> "One who has unreliable friends soon comes to ruin, but there is a friend who sticks closer than a brother."

Is Jesus your friend?

Oftentimes, when we face adversity in life, the first thing we do is get on the phone and we call people who are in a worse condition than us. We want to hear what they've got to say.

"Speak on my situation. Can you tell me what I'm supposed to do? I don't know."

I'll be honest: they don't know the answer either! However, what they will do is spread your business to everyone. They will use your adversity to become popular in somebody else's eyes. That's what messy people do.

What do you do in response? Remember that there are some things you just need to tell Jesus alone—keep that between you and him. I promise he won't tell anyone!

You must trust Jesus with your pain. Don't trust ordinary people. The Bible says that iron sharpens iron, sharpens iron (Proverbs 27:17). However, you've got to know when you're dealing with iron and when you're dealing with a stick.

Once again, I ask you: is Jesus your friend? He needs to be!

~ MOMENT OF REFLECTION ~

Who is Jesus to you? Do you believe what he says about what's in your box?

_____

_____

_____

_____

_____

_____

_____

_____

_____

_____

_____

_____

Chapter Three

Jesus Is a Savior!

The second thing Jesus should be to you is your savior. Let's look at Hebrews 2:16-18 (Amplified Bible Version). It says,

> "16For, as we all know, He (Christ) does not take hold of [the fallen] angels [to give them a helping hand], but He does take hold of [the fallen] descendants of Abraham [extending to them His hand of deliverance].
> 17Therefore, it was essential that He had to be made like His brothers (mankind) in every respect, so that He might [by experience] become a merciful and faithful High Priest in things related to God, to make atonement (propitiation) for the people's sins [thereby

9

wiping away the sin, satisfying divine justice, and providing a way of reconciliation between God and mankind]. 18Because He Himself [in His humanity] has suffered in being tempted, He is able to help and provide immediate assistance to those who are being tempted and exposed to suffering."

That's also very powerful! God put on a flesh suit, and came down here and said, "I've got to save my people. I'm going to give them the opportunity to allow me to be their savior."

Because to be honest, you can't save yourself. I'm only being honest! I may look different now, but I wasn't the same in earlier years, and I needed a savior! I just didn't know I needed one.

What's funny about this is that we as human beings think that we chose God... He chose us! He knew the day and the hour that you would cry out to him. He is faithful, because he answered that call! He should be your savior. You should understand that relationship with him. He is many things to us, but the most important thing that He is would be savior!

~ MOMENT OF REFLECTION ~

In what ways can you honor your savior with
what's in your box?

_____

_____

_____

_____

_____

_____

_____

_____

_____

_____

Chapter Four

Jesus Is King!

He's also the King! You've been taught about your kingdom authority. For that, we'll look at Luke 1:32-33:

> "[32]He will be great and will be called the Son of the Most High. The Lord God will give him the throne of his father David, [33]and he will reign over Jacob's descendants forever; his kingdom will never end."

Sometimes we've just got to put God back in His proper place. We put a lot of things in His place that we should not put there.

Real Housewives of whatever should not be there. Yes, I watched it! Afterwards, I go and I repent because of what I'd seen!

I say that to say that you've got to put God first. That means you got to carve out some time to spend with Him. Read about his kingdom! Read about who anointed him king!

~ MOMENT OF REFLECTION ~

What's in YOUR Box? What is it worth? If you
LOOK in your BOX, can you have MORE
abundance?

_____

_____

_____

_____

_____

_____

_____

_____

_____

_____

Chapter Five

Jesus Is Resurrection!

The next thing Jesus should be to you is the
resurrection. Let's look at Matthew 27:50-54
(NIV):

> "50And when Jesus had cried out again in a
> loud voice, he gave up his spirit. 51At that
> moment the curtain of the temple was torn in
> two from top to bottom. The earth shook, the
> rocks split 52 and the tombs broke open. The
> bodies of many holy people who had died
> were raised to life. 53They came out of the
> tombs after Jesus' resurrection and went into
> the holy city and appeared to many people
> 54When the centurion and those with him
> who were guarding Jesus saw the earthquake

and all that had happened, they were
terrified, and exclaimed, "Surely he was the
Son of God!"

When Jesus got up, the same stuff was buried in
the ground got up with him!

I'm going to let that sink in.

Imagine a family member of yours that passed
away. When you go outside, you see them
standing there as though nothing has happened.
That's the power of Jesus!

At that time, you knew that you no longer
confess your sins to any man. You confess them
to Jesus! You may not understand it, and there's
many that don't, but we'll go a bit deeper.

I'm from a traditional church, and at the time
that I got pregnant, I wasn't married. I was out
there, I told y'all. And I went back home, and
talked to my grandmother.

My grandmother was in a Baptist Church that
was small, it only had 12 people— 6 of them were
deacons, and 3 of them were ushers. They also
had someone for announcements, that was me.

Imagine being in a church, visibly pregnant and unmarried, giving announcements! I asked the people of the church to forgive me, as they knew I was pregnant. They all forgave me, but in a sense, that thinking is backwards.

I confessed my sin to them, but in actuality, the only one I needed to confess my sin to was Jesus. And He was there. He saw me when I did it.

To go a bit deeper, I'll let you in on a little secret. At that time, I didn't even know who Jesus was; I didn't know how to ask forgiveness! This is what led me to ask forgiveness from those that I thought needed to forgive me, the people that I could see.

In the spirit of resurrection, that resurrection power lives within us. If you walked in that power that's within you, you surely resurrect some dead things in your life! I'm just saying, Speak life into those dead things, those dead dreams, those family members that haven't come to Christ. Speak life on that! You must realize the power that's within you!

He is a friend, the savior, and resurrection. To Mary, He was all of those things. He was everything because, like I said before, she had a relationship with him. She spent time with him. She listened to him talk about the kingdom. She knew he was God. She knew that, so I want you to be encouraged. Speak to those things in your life. Put Jesus back in his proper place.

Stop putting it off; the world needs the church! They need us to stand up! They need what's in your box! You sit down at your job with your box closed, knowing full well that someone sitting next to you is going through adversity, and can use those words of life. We got to stop gorging ourselves on His word and keeping it to ourselves. There's so many people hurting and you can speak life into someone, but instead we speak death.

We're quick to judge others based on their outward appearance, and what we feel they should be doing. Tell that person (with love!) what needs to be done.

I wasn't always the best at this, but I had people by my side willing to help! The way I was headed, I probably wouldn't be standing here to be honest with you, but that's another story for another time.

~ MOMENT OF REFLECTION ~

What's in YOUR Box? Have you buried any gifts?
What can you do to use what is in your box for
his kingdom?

_____

_____

_____

_____

_____

_____

_____

_____

_____

_____

Chapter Six

Now Then, Back to You...

What's in your box?

Maybe you don't know what your box looks like. If not, I'll help you out. Your box can be your gifts. Are any of you reading this gifted? You should all be saying "yes!" If not, you're going to discover your gifts, because God will stir up your gifts. Your gift may be singing, dancing (especially praise dancing, I love it!), or ministering.

Your box can be your time. Do you have some time to give away on your job? Talk to somebody that needs to hear the Word! Give your time away!

Your box can also be your finances. I know a lot of times we think that our job is our source. Our job is NOT our source.

I'm going to say it again: Our job is NOT a source.

If we can get that through our heads, we can make time for Jesus left and right, as well as for the kingdom because you understand that your kingdom is your source. God is our source!

Truthfully, your job is a source for your seed. It's time to stop eating your seed and plant it, because that's part of your box.

Your tithes, your offerings, your first fruits; that's important! Social media would paint the church out to be something horrible, such as using Jesus to get money out of others.

If you go to see Jay Z or Beyonce in concert, you wouldn't ask if you could come in for free, would you? Think about that for a moment.

Even the Bible says that money answers all things (Ecclesiastes 10:19)! In that vein, I wouldn't understand why you would want your man of God to be in any less shape than what he provides for you! That man of God watches over your soul; why not bless him?

What is your box worth? What is your box? Why does it mean so much to you to hold on to the gifts that are in that box?

You have the gift of singing, why keep that to yourself? We hold on to our gifts with a death grip, when we can use them and speak life!

I hear you. I know we don't have time to really give God everything and we don't know what he really wants, but he wants sacrificial giving, that's all. Keep in mind, it's not just money that you can give! It could be clothing. You know somebody that needs some clothes? You know you can't fit those pants any longer, give them away! Give them away to somebody that can wear them. Believe me, it's okay, but that's a seed. Whatever you sow, God will continue to give back to you in that area. Mary didn't think twice about what her gift was worth, she just gave it!

I heard a minister say one time that a person can only give according to the amount of Word in them. So if you have not been in the Word, if you do not know who Jesus is, if you do not understand what sowing and reaping is, give what you can. If you continue to grow your spirit and feed it, that level of Word will grow, and you'll give away a check. I've done it before!

To be honest, I couldn't imagine my life without God. At times, it may seem like we can't give anything, because we're tired; we work and we're human, but to be honest, God gives us the supernatural strength. We need to do what He has called us to do.

I emphasize what he has called us to do; what you are anointed to do. If it's hard and you're suffering, that's not for you. It should flow effortlessly. Connect to the Source so that you can have your strength renewed and that way you can do those things. Regardless, they need to be done! People have to know about Christ. We have to win souls. It's more to just coming to the church, it is something we have to do outside of these walls.

Now let me ask you this: Are you concerned with somebody else's box? You can't know what's in your box because you're looking at somebody else's box!

This was how Judas thought. He was more concerned with selling the oil to feed the poor —though we know he had ulterior motives!

Though it brings an interesting thing to light. Sometimes somebody else's box will make us embarrassed because we don't have anything in ours, but that's okay. At least you have a box!

You can pull something out of that. Connect with Jesus so he can show you what to do... it's that simple! You don't have to be envious of somebody else's gifts! There's enough work in the body for everybody to reap the benefits! With that, I have one final question (next chapter).

~ MOMENT OF REFLECTION ~

What's in YOUR Box? Have you had any ideas in the past of things you would like to do with your life?

_____

_____

_____

_____

_____

_____

_____

_____

_____

_____

Chapter Seven

What Will Jesus Remember About Your Box?

What will he remember about the contents of your box? The Word says that Jesus was so moved by Mary's gift to him, and another scripture said that her act will be remembered forever.

What will Jesus remember about our box? What will he say about our praise, about our service? He remembers our service! When you get talked into doing something you don't want to do, and the person you think isn't looking turns away, you start grumbling and griping. Jesus sees these things.

The children of Israel were swallowed into the ground, griping and grumbling about the kingdom work. Jesus is going to remember something, so why not just make the commitment? Let's just say, "Okay Lord, whatever you want to do with me, I'll do it. Wherever you want me to go, I'll be there."

It's hard to work in the Kingdom of God; it's hard to do it by yourself. Discover what's in your box, cultivate it, and connect to the source with Jesus in his proper place. Set the tone; get things right so that you can continue to grow. You can't walk in that authority that is constantly talked about in the church unless you recognize that you have a box, and know what's in it.

~ *The End* ~

~ MOMENT OF REFLECTION ~

What will Jesus remember about YOUR box? If
you are NOT happy with what he will remember,
what can you do NOW to change it?

_____

_____

_____

_____

_____

_____

_____

_____

_____

_____

~ NOTES ~

_____

_____

_____

_____

_____

_____

_____

_____

_____

_____

~ NOTES ~

_____

_____

_____

_____

_____

_____

_____

_____

_____

_____

_____

~ NOTES ~

_____

_____

_____

_____

_____

_____

_____

_____

_____

_____

Thank you for your support!

As a gift to you, I would love to share this video
with you as a token of my appreciation:

Bit.ly/yourbox2018

Made in the USA
Columbia, SC
25 November 2024

47512578R00026